VOICES & CHOICES

331

VOICES & CHOICES

Struggling with Temptation

Donald L. Deffner

Publishing House
St. Louis

Cover photo: M. L. Brubaker

Copyright © 1984 Concordia Publishing House
3558 South Jefferson Avenue, St. Louis, MO 63118-3968
Manufactured in the United States of America

Library of Congress Cataloging in Publication Data
Deffner, Donald L.
    Voices and choices.

       1. Christian life—1960-   2. Temptation.
I. Title.
BV4501.2.D429   1984   242   84-7050
ISBN 0-570-03939-8 (pbk.)

1 2 3 4 5 6 7 8 9 10 SP 93 92 91 90 89 88 87 86 85 84

To my brother
Richard Paul Deffner

Contents

Introduction   12

The Voice talks about—
    Being Your Real Self
"In this cruel world the only person you can really
count on is yourself! Right?"
    Feeling Drained?   15
    How Modest!   16
    Resisting Pressure   17
    Freedom Now!   18

The Voice talks about—
    Keeping Your Charm
"Don't change. God loves you just the way you
are."
    Great Expectations   21
    Fame   22

The Voice talks about—
    Poise, Pride, and Persistence
"It's heartwarming to be a little bit above the crowd,
don't you think?"
    Three Categories   24
    "I've Had a Hard Life"   25

The Voice talks about—
    Self-Control
"Thank God you are one of those *balanced* individuals who has learned to be *in* the world but not *of*
it! Congratulations!"

Trust vs. Naiveté   28
Living Alone   29
The Balancing Act   30

The Voice talks about—
    Dealing with Emotions
"You've suffered so much more than many people I know. You have my sympathy!"

    I'm So Sorry!   33
    Questions   34

The Voice talks about—
    Handling Frustration
"How important your time is! Why don't people learn more respect for another person's schedules?"

    How Can I Pray?   37
    Don't Touch?   38
    Beep! Beep!   39
    It's Not Your Fault   40

The Voice talks about—
    Just Hanging In There
"How can you fabricate a feeling of happiness when you are in the depths of despair?"

    Me Feel Happy? Ha!   42
    You're Pretty Good   43

The Voice talks about—
    Developing Your Own Life-Style
"Concentrate on developing those intrinsic qualities and you will be blessed and be a blessing to others."

    Your Hidden Talents   46
    Retreat!   47

Relaxed Evangelism 48
Living Alone and Liking It 49

The Voice talks about—
Clever Communication
"What's wrong with an occasional dart dipped in sarcasm to make your point while sparring with your partner? Are you just a carpet to be walked on?"

Fruitful Arguments 52
Choosing the Right Friends 53
Cracks in the Armor 54
Did You Hear? 55
How Rude! 56
A Fine Command of Language 58
Open Up! 59
Darts Dipped in Sarcasm 60

The Voice talks about—
Intimate Relationships
"Who is trying to control you at work or at home as if your time, your talents, and your feelings are their possessions? How insensitive the ones we love can be to us at times. Don't you think so?"

The Art of Silence 62
"Why Did You...?" 63
Who's in Control? 64
Learning the Art of Self-Dependence 65
Me—Jealous? Never! 66

The Voice talks about—
Getting Ahead in Life
"One has to learn how to adapt. Right? This is the 20th century. One must be *realistic*!"

One Must Be *Realistic* 69
Submission 70

On Wielding Power 71
Lifeless Garden Hoses? 72
You Can Do It! 73
Just a Job 75
"Moving On Up!" 75

The Voice talks about—
Doing All Right with God
"I think some people can make you *feel* bad when you really haven't done anything *that* bad at all. Shake off those negative feelings. Don't be so hard on yourself. Enjoy God's gift of a happy life for you."

Pray for the Poor 78
Doing OK with God 79
Loosen Up! 80
Congratulations! 82
They Blew It 82

The Voice talks about—
Those Overcommitted Christians
"Some Christians may have it easy with their little faith formulas. But life is tough. Hang in there. You've got *my* sympathy."

Busyness, Bazaars, and Building Programs 86
Share More of Yourself 87
GOD IS LOVE! 88
You Are Not Albert Schweitzer 89
Faith Formulas 91

The Voice talks about—
Considering Divorce
"Why not admit you can never be what the other person wants you to be? Why feel you can never be any good with anyone else if you couldn't make it with your partner?"

I Don't Need Counseling 94
1 + 1 = 1? 95
The Fire in the Bedroom 96
Fulfillment Outside Your Marriage 97
Time for Divorce? 99

The Voice talks about—
        The Past, Present, and Future
"The debris of the past in the river of your life is not necessarily of your own making. So live with yourself as you are. Don't try to be something you are not. *Be you!*"

Happiness Is Coming Your Way! 102
Quiet Dignified Resignation 103
Facing Death? 104
Change for the Sake of Change? 105
Think on Things Eternal 106

The Voice talks about—
        Coping with the Daily Drag
"How you tire of everyone around you who wants to use you for selfish purposes and designs! What new opportunity beckons you? Where is the fresh start you so richly deserve?"

Waiting for Help 109
Family Devotions 110
They Just Don't Understand 111
Tired? Move Out! 112
Most Sincerely Yours—*The Voice* 113

Epilog: The Christian Responds 115

Author's Postscript to the Reader 117

Further Uses for This Book 119

Reflections 122

Introduction

The scene was a small midweek gathering at a church in the suburbs. The members of the group had been discussing *I Hear Two Voices: Struggling with Temptation* (the predecessor to this volume). Upon reading the opening piece spoken by *The Voice* (the Tempter) one woman said, "Well, that sounds pretty good to me! That's the way I feel."

And then the discussion began. Because what *The Voice* says within the hearts of so many of us sounds so "right," so in tune with our own (often self-centered) feelings and the culture around us, we are moved to agree with it. And the subtle thing is that what *The Voice* says has some truth in it. But that is the deceptive part. For it is a *half*-truth—and therefore a *lie.* And it is our task as Christians—by the grace of the Holy Spirit and in the light of God's Holy Word—to discern the difference between truth and falsehood—not that that decision is easily made in a complex, modern society.

God calls us to decide and act every day in relation to each ethical dilemma we encounter. The blessed truth is that God in Christ does not leave us helpless or comfortless in our quandary. He does *act* with His Holy Spirit and empowers us to make the right decision. He promises:

> Every test that you have experienced is the kind that normally comes to people. But God keeps His promise, and He will not allow you to be tested beyond your power to remain firm; at the time you are put to the test, He will give

you the strength to endure it, and so provide you with a way out (1 Corinthians 10:13 TEV).

And the resources of this power to escape and conquer temptation are in His Word. The means of receiving His grace are further in our Baptism and the Eucharist and in a vigorous life of prayer and the enriching fellowship of other Christians.

When we are in touch with the Source, the divine power supply, then we need not fear the clever, wooing, and demonic call of *The Voice*.

Here then are some more of the voices that whisper within us every day. I have heard many of them. Have you?

Confront them. Recognize them for what they are. But know that you are not alone in your struggle. The Christ who died for you on the cross—and rose again—has conquered the Tempter. And you can recognize that *Voice* and challenge it with Christ's own words: "Go away, Satan." In your personal, daily life you can realize the fulfillment of God's promise: "Resist the devil, and he will run away from you" (James 4:7 TEV).

In a number of places there are references to the "Reflections" in the back of the book. These will give some further insights.

Now may God go with you in your struggle, and may the Holy Spirit guide you in your response.

The Voice talks about—

Being Your Real Self

"In this cruel world the only person you can really count on is *yourself!* Right?"

Feeling Drained?

The Voice: When you see
how other people
use you
cheat you
manipulate you
malign you
refuse to lend you
a helping hand
it's a real drag
isn't it?
It makes one realize
that ultimately
in this cruel world
the only person
you can really
count on
is
yourself!
Right?
I'm with you!

But *Another Voice* said:

Know ye that the Lord He is God: it is He that hath made us and not we ourselves (Psalm 100:3 KJV). Let us run with determination the race that lies before us. Let us keep our eyes fixed on Jesus, on whom our faith depends from beginning to end. He did not give up because of the cross! On the contrary, because of the joy that was waiting for him, He thought nothing of the disgrace of dying on the cross, and He is now seated at the right side of God's throne (Hebrews 12:1-2 TEV).

How Modest

The Voice: *I heard*
   a great man
   once say
   that one of the things
   we need the most
   is more
   modesty
   I think that
   is quite profound
   I suggest
   that you and I
   work on that
   Becoming more modest
   And I think
   other people
   will soon notice
   how modest
   you and I have
   become

But *Another Voice* said:

If someone thinks he is something when he really is nothing, he is only deceiving himself (Galatians 6:3 TEV). People who are proud will soon be disgraced. It is wiser to be modest (Proverbs 11:2 TEV). Never let yourself think that you are wiser than you are; simply obey the Lord and refuse to do wrong (Proverbs 3:7 TEV).

(See Reflection 1)

Resisting Pressure

The Voice: *Don't let your partner*
push you into becoming
something you are not
(like some other person
he or she really admires)
Rather
A reserved humility
on your part suggests
that you be
the relaxed
genuine person
that you are
So resist the pressure
to achieve the impossible
or to alter your personality
or to change and subvert
the real "you"
Be the person
God intended
you to be

But *Another Voice* said:
Lazy people should learn a lesson from the way ants live. They have no leader, chief, or ruler, but they store up their food during the summer, getting ready for winter.

How long is the lazy man going to lie around? (Proverbs 6:6-9 TEV).

The Spirit that God has given us does not make us timid; instead, His Spirit fills us with power, love, and self-control (2 Timothy 1:7 TEV). Grow in grace, and in the knowledge of our Lord and Savior Jesus Christ. To Him be glory both now and forever (2 Peter 3:18 KJV).

Freedom Now!

The Voice: What bondage
are you in?
What's keeping
you down?
What's inhibiting you
from expressing
the real inner you
in marriage?
at work?
at school?
in the groups
you belong to?
Express yourself!
Assert your independence
in Christ!
Be the freed person
God wants you
to be

But *Another Voice* said:

Because of God's great mercy to us I appeal to you: Offer yourselves as a living sacrifice to God, dedicated to

His service and pleasing to Him. This is the true worship that you should offer (Romans 12:1 TEV). Look out for one another's interests, not just for your own. The attitude you should have is the one that Christ Jesus had. . . . Of His own free will He gave up all He had, and took the nature of a servant. . . . Keep on working with fear and trembling to complete your salvation, because God is always at work in you to make you willing and able to obey His own purpose (Philippians 2:4-5, 7, 12-13 TEV).

The Voice talks about—

Keeping Your Charm

"Don't change. God loves you just the way you are."

Great Expectations

The Voice: I am incredibly
intuitive
when it comes
to gauging
the inherent qualities
in a person
Well
you have it
I just don't think
you've really found
your niche yet
Be patient
(I'm on your side)
Your potentiality
is yet to be realized
and the world
will know
who you
really
are

But *Another Voice* said:
We are to use our different gifts in accordance with the grace that God has given us (Romans 12:6 TEV). There are different kinds of spiritual gifts, but the same Spirit gives them. There are different ways of serving, but the same Lord is served (1 Corinthians 12:4 TEV). Be satisfied with what you have (Hebrews 13:5 TEV).

21

Fame

The Voice: Why is it that
others seem
to receive the cheers
and you the jeers?
Others achieve fame
and you are a
no-name?
I don't think
you are fully appreciated
You can justly
be proud
of your achievements
Take heart
God knows

But *Another Voice* said:

If one of you wants to be great, he must be the servant of the rest (Matthew 20:26 TEV). What [the Lord] requires of us is this: to do what is just, to show constant love, and to live in humble fellowship with our God (Micah 6:8 TEV). Do not work for food that spoils; instead, work for the food that lasts for eternal life (John 6:27 TEV). Be concerned above everything else with the kingdom of God and with what He requires of you (Matthew 6:33 TEV).

The Voice talks about—

Poise, Pride, and Persistence

"It's heartwarming to be a little bit above the crowd, don't you think?"

Three Categories

The Voice: How absolutely
   BORING
   some people can be
   chattering away
   about what interests them
   the most
   Now
   I say
   people talk
   about three basic things
   Other people
   Events and
   Ideas
   I'm in the
   latter category
   like you!
   It's heartwarming
   to be
   a little bit
   above the crowd
   don't you think?

But *Another Voice* said:

Wicked people are controlled by their conceit and arrogance, and this is sinful (Proverbs 21:4 TEV). Do not be proud, but accept humble duties. Do not think of yourselves as wise (Romans 12:16 TEV). If someone thinks he is something when he really is nothing, he is only deceiving himself (Galatians 6:3 TEV). Let this mind be in you, which was also in Christ Jesus (Philippians 2:5 KJV).

"I've Had a Hard Life"

The Voice: From your study
of the Bible
wouldn't you agree
that the Christian
should sort of
welcome or at least
expect pain
and testing?
Not masochistically
of course
But it is a sign
(so the Bible says)
that you are one
of God's special children
singled out
for trials
And that can give you
a certain pride
and dignity
that others
don't have
(whose lives
are so easy)

But *Another Voice* said:

Pride leads to destruction, and arrogance to downfall (Proverbs 16:18 TEV). Do not think of yourself more highly than you should. Instead, be modest in your thinking, and judge yourself according to the amount of faith that God has given you (Romans 12:3 TEV). Humble yourselves before the Lord, and He will lift you up (James 4:10 TEV).

The Voice talks about—

Self-Control

"Thank God you are one of those *balanced* individuals who has learned to be *in* the world but not *of* it! Congratulations!"

Trust vs. Naiveté

The Voice: There's a difference
between trust
and naivete
Wanting to be kind
to others
and leaving yourself
wide open
to be manipulated
Wisdom is called for
We live in a cruel
and hostile world
We all
are sinners
and prone to
exploitation
by other people
So learn to practice
a wary and thoughtful
defense
in your life
and you
will be known as
a person of
real integrity

But *Another Voice* said:
Do you, my friend, pass judgment on others?...Do
you think you will escape God's judgment? Or perhaps

you despise His great kindness, tolerance, and patience. Surely you know that God is kind, because He is trying to lead you to repent (Romans 2:1, 3-4 TEV). If someone has done you wrong, do not repay him with a wrong. Try to do what everyone considers to be good. Do everything possible on your part to live in peace with everybody.... Do not let evil defeat you; instead, conquer evil with good (Romans 12:17-18, 21 TEV).

Living Alone

*The Voice: Ultimately we live
very much within
ourselves
All a preacher
can really do
is direct you
to God's Word
A counselor
is not there
to "give answers"
but to help you
create and live with
your own decisions
So you're really
on your own
That's not so bad
God is aware
of your loneliness
Go to Him
with your problems
His door
is always
open*

But *Another Voice* said:

Your life in Christ makes you strong, and His love comforts you. You have fellowship with the Spirit, and you have kindness and compassion for one another.... Look out for one another's interests, not just for your own (Philippians 2:1,4 TEV). Is anyone among you in trouble?...He should send for the church elders, who will pray for him (James 5:13-14 TEV).

The Balancing Act

The Voice: It's good to see
      you are not
      one of those
      "master achievers"
      in society
      driven by
      greed
      lust
      power
      wealth
      revenge
      success!
      Thank God
      you are one of those
      balanced *individuals*
      who has learned
      to be in *the world*
      but not of *it*
      Congratulations!
      Keep up that
      fine balance

But *Another Voice* said:
The Lord sees everything you do. Wherever you go, He is watching (Proverbs 5:21 TEV). Can you carry fire against your chest without burning your clothes? Can you walk on hot coals without burning your feet? (Proverbs 6:27-28 TEV). What you think is the right road may lead to death (Proverbs 14:12 TEV). You may think that everything you do is right, but the Lord judges your motives (Proverbs 21:2 TEV).

(See Reflection 2)

The Voice talks about—

Dealing with Emotions

"You've suffered so much more than many people I know. You have my sympathy!"

I'm So Sorry!

The Voice: You've suffered
so much more
than many people
I know
Oh maybe not always
physical anguish
but mental torture
and inner trials
You have my sympathy!
If only others
around you
knew what you
have gone through
Then they would
appreciate you more
You certainly have
my admiration!

But *Another Voice* said:

Regard not lightly the chastening of the Lord, nor faint when thou art reproved of Him; for whom the Lord loveth He chasteneth, and scourgeth every son whom He receiveth.... God corrects us for our own benefit, so that we may share in His holiness. Now obviously no "chastening" seems pleasant at the time: it is in fact most unpleasant. Yet when it is all over we can see that it has quietly produced the fruit of real goodness in the

33

characters of those who have accepted it. So tighten your loosening grip (Hebrews 12:5-6, 10-12 Phillips).

Questions

The Voice: Aren't there times
when you wonder
about what
is really true?
Who you really are?
Where you are headed?
Whether people really *care*
for you?
What the purpose and meaning
of your life
is ultimately
all about?
Now don't feel guilty
about those questions
The greatest saints
in history
have had them
So I say
pursue those questions
and nourish your doubt
for you will be
a wiser
and more mature person
as a result

But *Another Voice* said:

O ye of little faith (Matthew 6:30 KJV). I know whom I have believed, and am persuaded that He is able to keep that which I have committed unto Him against that day (2 Timothy 1:12 KJV). If any of you lacks wisdom, he should pray to God, who will give it to him; because God gives generously and graciously to all. But when you pray, you must believe and not doubt at all. Whoever doubts is like a wave in the sea that is driven and blown about by the wind. A person like that, unable to make up his mind and undecided in all he does, must not think that he will receive anything from the Lord (James 1:5-7 TEV).

The Voice talks about—

Handling Frustration

"How important your time is! Why don't people learn more respect for another person's schedules?"

How Can I Pray?

The Voice: It's hard
to pray
in a vacuum
isn't it?
When you feel
lonely
despairing
down
drained
How can one pray?
Pray! (they say)
It's just not
that easy

But *Another Voice* said:

Then shalt thou call, and the Lord shall answer; thou shalt cry, and He shall say, Here I am (Isaiah 58:9 KJV). It shall come to pass, that before they call, I will answer; and while they are yet speaking I will hear (Isaiah 65:24 KJV). Ask, and it shall be given you; seek, and ye shall find; knock, and it shall be opened unto you (Luke 11:9 KJV).

(See Reflection 3)

Don't Touch?

The Voice: I am sure you
hardly think of yourself
as a person
without sexual feelings
(even at your present age
and even if
you are in
the mature years)
So I affirm
your ongoing appreciation
for a handsome man
or a beautiful woman
God didn't create
a lovely person
and then say
"Don't look!"
or
"You can see
but
Don't touch!"
I think He wants us
to enjoy
each other
God put
sexual desires
into our hearts
A kiss
A touch
An embrace
They're all
a natural expression
of our God-given
human emotions

But *Another Voice* said:
Anyone who looks at a woman and wants to possess her is guilty of committing adultery with her in his heart (Matthew 5:28 TEV). To be controlled by human nature results in death; to be controlled by the Spirit results in life and peace (Romans 8:6 TEV).

Beep! Beep!

The Voice: I always
beep my horn twice—
a polite signal
to a driver
who is moving
too slowly
(Dangerous!)
(Always follow the flow
of traffic!)
Don't you agree?
Why can't drivers
learn more respect
for others' schedules
and appointments
and
move over?!
Let's start
a campaign
you and me
Two beeps
and there'll be
fewer creeps
on the highway

But *Another Voice* said:

Help the weak, be patient with everyone. See that no one pays back wrong for wrong, but at all times make it your aim to do good to one another and to all people (1 Thessalonians 5:14-15 TEV).

It's Not Your Fault

The Voice: Your disenchantment
despair
disillusionment
doubt
defeat
may well not be
your fault at all
but rather
physiological in nature
You are just
going through
the process
of aging
(Don't we all?)
It will pass
Things will get better
You've certainly got
my sympathy

But *Another Voice* said:

Why am I so sad? Why am I so troubled? I will put my hope in God, and once again I will praise Him, my Savior and my God (Psalm 42:5 TEV).

(See Reflection 4)

The Voice talks about—

Just Hanging in There

"How can you fabricate a feeling of happiness when you are in the depths of despair?"

Me Feel Happy? Ha!

The Voice: I think
there's a great deal
to be sad
and unhappy about
in this day and age
And in your
personal life also
Right?
I know
how you have suffered
How can a person
fabricate a feeling
of happiness
when you are
in the depths of
despair?
That
is
just
plain
idiotic

But *Another Voice* said:

Being cheerful keeps you healthy. It is slow death to be gloomy all the time (Proverbs 17:22 TEV). Call to Me when trouble comes; I will save you, and you will praise Me (Psalm 50:15 TEV). Do not be surprised at the painful test you are suffering, as though something unusual were happening to you. Rather be glad that you are sharing Christ's sufferings, so that you may be full of joy when His glory is revealed (1 Peter 4:12-13 TEV).

(See Reflection 5)

You're Pretty Good

The Voice: I know you
have never been guilty
of murder
robbery
rape
embezzlement
or other such
heinous crimes
as some people have
So although you and I
do slip and fall
occasionally
in "small" sins
(who doesn't
make a mistake
now and then?)
we shouldn't live
in guilt or fear
but in the relaxed
calm certainty
of God's protection
He loves
His erring children
He is a forgiving God
So don't be
too hard

on yourself
You are a
pretty good person
after all

But *Another Voice* said:
Whoever breaks one commandment is guilty of breaking them all (James 2:10 TEV). Can anyone really say that his conscience is clear, that he has gotten rid of his sin? (Proverbs 20:9 TEV). I know that in me (that is, in my flesh) dwelleth no good thing (Romans 7:18 KJV). Thanks be to God who gives us the victory through our Lord Jesus Christ! (1 Corinthians 15:57 TEV).

The Voice talks about—

Developing Your Own Life-Style

"Concentrate on developing those intrinsic qualities and you will be blessed and be a blessing to others."

Your Hidden Talents

The Voice: I think
    it is very important
    to experience
    the feelings
    God has placed inside you
    love
    courage
    forgiveness
    patience
    tenderness
    kindness
    courtesy
    (the real inner you)
    So in your prayers
    meditate on
    your inner being
    Concentrate on
    developing those
    intrinsic qualities
    and you
    will be blessed
    and be
    a blessing
    to others

But *Another Voice* said:
    By grace are ye saved through faith; and that not of yourselves: it is the gift of God: not of works, lest any

man should boast. For we are His workmanship, created in Christ Jesus unto good works, which God hath before ordained that we should walk in them (Ephesians 2:8-10 KJV). Without Me ye can do nothing (John 15:5 KJV).

(See Reflection 6)

Retreat!

The Voice: Christ often retreated
to a quiet place
to rest and pray
I think
there are times
we need to withdraw
from others
to learn the art
of living with
oneself
Other people need to learn
self-dependence
and not always use
you
You need
your own
space
So feel free
to take off
like Jesus
and do
your
own
thing

But *Another Voice* said:
Do not think of yourself more highly than you should. Instead, be modest in your thinking, and judge yourself according to the amount of faith that God has given you (Romans 12:3 TEV). Accept one another...for the glory of God, as Christ has accepted you (Romans 15:7 TEV). Where two or three come together in My name, I am there with them (Matthew 18:20 TEV).

Relaxed Evangelism

The Voice: As I recall it
Christ never went around
in His
three-year ministry
compulsive
nervous and pushy
like I see
some of these
"overcommitted Christians"
today
I say we need
to "cool it"
in our Christian
witnessing
Let others have
a different
point of view
The truth
needs no defense
Right?

But *Another Voice* said:

We cannot stop speaking of what we ourselves have seen and heard (Acts 4:20 TEV). I am not ashamed of the Gospel: it is the power of God for salvation to every one who has faith (Romans 1:16 RSV). I heard the Lord say, "Whom shall I send? Who will be Our messenger?" I answered, "I will go! Send me!" (Isaiah 6:8 TEV).

Living Alone and Liking It

The Voice: *Just try sharing*
your private hopes and dreams
with someone else
and see where it gets you
You'll probably
hear it back
from a
"well-meaning friend"
in three weeks
I say
maintain your privacy
Learn the dignity
of thoughtful solitude
You are special
in God's eyes
Be *special*
Some of the greatest
artists composers writers
thinkers builders geniuses
learned to live alone
and like it

But *Another Voice* said:

If you do not forgive others, your Father in heaven will not forgive the wrongs you have done (Mark 11:26 TEV). We who are strong in the faith ought to help the weak to carry their burdens. We should not please ourselves. Instead, we should all please our brothers for their own good, in order to build them up in the faith. ...And may God, the source of patience and encouragement, enable you to have the same point of view among yourselves by following the example of Christ Jesus, so that all of you together may praise with one voice the God and Father of our Lord Jesus Christ (Romans 15:1-2, 5-6 TEV).

The Voice talks about—

Clever Communication

"What's wrong with an occasional dart dipped in sarcasm to make your point while sparring with your partner? Are you just a carpet to be walked on?"

Fruitful Arguments

The Voice: They bragged
that they had
50 years of marriage
without a quarrel
How consummately boring!
Psychiatrists say
arguments can be
fruitful and
productive
For our inner
feelings and resentments
are not to be suppressed
but expressed
and coped with
So I say
misunderstandings
can be
fruitful arenas
for mutual growth
Be honest about
your true feelings
Don't just
drift through
decades of
bland existence
Live!

But *Another Voice* said:
   If you stay calm, you are wise, but if you have a hot temper, you only show how stupid you are (Proverbs 14:29 TEV). Patience brings peace (Proverbs 15:18 TEV). Get rid of all these things: anger, passion, and hateful feelings. No insults or obscene talk must ever come from your lips (Colossians 3:8 TEV). You have fellowship with the Spirit, and you have kindness and compassion for one another (Philippians 2:1 TEV).

Choosing the Right Friends

The Voice: Some people are always
           negative
           They always take the opposite
           point of view
           They are experts on
           one-upmanship
           (Have you had an experience?
           Wait till you hear theirs!)
           What shall we do
           with these people?
           Will listening
           help them mature?
           I doubt it
           I suggest
           quiet withdrawal
           Seek the company
           of more mature
           individuals
           who readily
           appreciate
           your insights
           and understandings

Learn how to gauge
the type of company
you keep
where dialog can be
mutually
productive

But *Another Voice* said:
Do you, my friend, pass judgment on others? You have no excuse at all, whoever you are. For when you judge others, and then do the same things which they do, you condemn yourself (Romans 2:1 TEV). Be patient with everyone (1 Thessalonians 5:14 TEV). Be kind to each other, be compassionate. Be as ready to forgive others as God for Christ's sake has forgiven you (Ephesians 4:32 Phillips).

Cracks in the Armor

The Voice: *Next time*
you're in
a disagreement
a quarrel
a fight
Hold back
Keep calm
Let the other person
lose control
Not you
That's a sign
of maturity
Look for

the cracks
in the other person's
armor
Your time
will come

But *Another Voice* said:
 If someone has done you wrong, do not repay him with a wrong. Try to do what everyone considers good. Do everything possible, on your part, to live at peace with everybody....Do not let evil defeat you; instead, conquer evil with good (Romans 12:17-18, 21 TEV). God's peace, which is far beyond human understanding, will keep your hearts and minds safe in union with Christ Jesus (Philippians 4:7 TEV).

Did You Hear?

The Voice: You and I
   know what gossip is
   and Scripture says
   to avoid it
   Nevertheless
   there are times
   (don't you agree?)
   that it's necessary
   to pass on helpful information
   to a trusted friend
   so somebody else
   can be helped
   for their own good
   Sound advice
   from a person

of maturity
like you
is one thing
Gossip
is
another

But *Another Voice* said:

Gossip is so tasty—how we love to swallow it! (Proverbs 18:8 TEV). Righteous people speak wisdom, but the tongue that speaks evil will be stopped. Righteous people know the kind thing to say, but the wicked are always saying things that hurt (Proverbs 10:31-32 TEV). Be careful what you say and protect your life. A careless talker destroys himself (Proverbs 13:3 TEV). What you say can preserve life or destroy it; so you must accept the consequences of your words (Proverbs 18:21 TEV). May God, the source of patience and encouragement, enable you to have the same point of view among yourselves by following the example of Jesus Christ, so that all of you together may praise with one voice the God and Father of our Lord Jesus Christ (Romans 15:5-6 TEV).

How Rude!

The Voice: Have you noticed
how some people
start talking
in the middle
of your sentence
(before you've finished
a completed thought)

And they *call* that
"conversation"!
How rude!
As if they knew
all
you were going
to say!
Next time
try this
Just keep talking
while`raising your voice
a little
and watch
their eyes widen
as you make
your point
Then they may learn
what "conversation"
is all about!

But *Another Voice* said:
Don't say, "I'll do to him just what he did to me! I'll get even with him!" (Proverbs 24:29 TEV). Listen before you answer. If you don't, you are being stupid and insulting (Proverbs 18:13 TEV). A wise, mature person is known for his understanding. The more pleasant his words, the more persuasive he is. Wisdom is a fountain of life to the wise, but trying to educate stupid people is a waste of time. Intelligent people think before they speak; what they say is then more persuasive. Kind words are like honey—sweet to the taste and good for your health (Proverbs 16:21-24 TEV).

(See Reflection 7)

A Fine Command of Language

The Voice: "It often shows
a fine command
of language
to say nothing"
goes the saying
So don't feel compulsive
about pushing your faith
on others
Respect their own
point of view
You are not responsible
for their salvation
They *are*
A time will come
in the future
when you can share
your point of view
So relax
Learn the art
of responsible
listening
and reflection

But *Another Voice* said:
   "You are My witnesses," [says the Lord] (Isaiah 43:10
RSV). Have reverence for Christ in your hearts, and honor
Him as Lord. Be ready at all times to answer anyone who
asks you to explain the hope you have in you, but do it
with gentleness and respect (1 Peter 3:15-16 TEV). The
message about repentance and the forgiveness of sins
must be preached to all nations, beginning in Jerusalem
(Luke 24:47 TEV).

(See Reflection 8)

Open Up!

The Voice: Much as you
wish to please
your partner
and respect
his or her expectations
do not deny
your unique individuality
your integrity
Be open
about your feelings
Let the real
inner you
be known
Feel free
to express
your inmost thoughts
For that's what
communication
is all about
Right?

But *Another Voice* said:

Stupid people always think they are right. Wise people listen to advice (Proverbs 12:15 TEV). Remember this....Everyone must be quick to listen, but slow to speak and slow to become angry (James 1:19 TEV). By speaking the truth in a spirit of love, we must grow up in every way to Christ, who is the Head (Ephesians 4:15 TEV).

Darts Dipped in Sarcasm

The Voice: What's wrong
with an occasional
dart dipped in sarcasm
to make your point
while sparring with
your partner
over a misunderstanding?
It's all in
good fun
isn't it?
Are you a carpet
to be walked on?
Does a relationship
with another person
mean the total submerging
of your unique personality?
I believe one has to
stand up for one's own
point of view and
challenge another's misconception
of where the truth
really lies
It can be fun
A game
of mutual growth

But *Another Voice* said:

Thoughtless words can wound as deeply as any sword, but wisely spoken words can heal. A lie has a short life, but truth lives on forever. Those who plan evil are in for a rude surprise, but those who work for good will find happiness (Proverbs 12:18-20 TEV).

The Voice talks about—

Intimate Relationships

"Who is trying to control you at work or at home as if your time, your talents, and your feelings are their possessions? How insensitive the ones we love can be to us at times. Don't you think so?"

The Art of Silence

The Voice: The use of silence
  in a relationship
  can be
  quite fruitful
  For one thing
  it gives your partner
  the chance to
  think things over
  and better see
  the mistake
  he or she made
  Always talking
  can be fruitless
  redundant
  counterproductive
  So learn the art
  of silence
  As Scripture says
  "Be slow to speak"

But *Another Voice* said:

Your speech should always be pleasant and interesting, and you should know how to give the right answer to everyone (Colossians 4:6 TEV). Rid yourselves...of all evil; no more lying or hypocrisy or jealousy or insulting language (1 Peter 2:1 TEV). An idea well expressed is like a design of gold, set in silver (Proverbs 25:11 TEV).

"Why Did You...?"

The Voice: How insensitive
other people
can be!
"Why did you do it
that way?"
or
"Now what you
should have done was . . ."
And they're the last
ever to say
"I'm sorry"
How can we
cope with them?
I suggest
withdrawal
No need to provoke
the other person
and cause a big
argument
They won't change anyway
Learn patience
and quietly tap
the inner confidence
of your own sound judgment
That shows wisdom
and maturity

But *Another Voice* said:

If your brother sins against you, go to him and show him his fault. But do it privately, just between yourselves. If he listens to you, you have won your brother back (Matthew 18:15 TEV). Love must be completely sincere

(Romans 12:9 TEV). Love never gives up; and its faith, hope, and patience never fail (1 Corinthians 13:7 TEV).

Who's in Control?

The Voice: Who is
> *trying to*
> *control you*
> *at work*
> *or at home*
> *as if your time*
> *your talents*
> *your feelings*
> *are their possessions?*
> *You are*
> *your own person*
> *Demand your freedom then*
> *God gave it*
> *to you*
> *Be*
> *your*
> *own*
> *person*

But *Another Voice* said:

"I am the vine, and you are the branches. Whoever remains in Me, and I in him, will bear much fruit; for you can do nothing without Me" (John 15:5 TEV). You do not belong to yourselves but to God (1 Corinthians 6:19 TEV). It is no longer I who live, but it is Christ who lives in me (Galatians 2:20 TEV). Whenever you possibly can, do good to those who need it (Proverbs 3:27 TEV). Help carry one another's burdens, and in this way you will obey the law of Christ (Galatians 6:2 TEV).

Learning the Art of Self-Dependence

The Voice: Do you sense
            at times
            that people
            don't really care
            about you?
            At least not
            the way
            they used to
            And after all
            the "reaching out"
            to others
            you have done
            in your life!
            Well
            I guess there's a time
            we all need
            to learn how to
            step back
            and live with ourselves
            It's painful
            but necessary
            Then one can learn
            the art of self-dependence
            and not depend
            on others
            (How insensitive
            people
            can be!)

But *Another Voice* said:

When you stand and pray, forgive anything you may have against anyone, so that your Father in heaven will forgive the wrongs you have done (Mark 11:25 TEV). If he sins against you seven times in one day, and each time he comes to you saying, "I repent," you must forgive him (Luke 17:4 TEV). Be kind and tenderhearted to one another, as God has forgiven you through Christ (Ephesians 4:32 TEV). Be tolerant with one another (Colossians 3:13 TEV). Do everything possible on your part to live in peace with everybody (Romans 12:18 TEV).

Me—Jealous? Never!

The Voice: When the one
you love
seems to
find enjoyment
with someone else
more than with you
That's the time
to be hurt
Isn't it?
("You always hurt
the one you love")
I think there's a place
for righteous anger
when that's happening
(That's Biblical)
Now jealousy
is quite something else
again
How insensitive

the ones we love
can be to us
at times
Don't you
think so?

But *Another Voice* said:
Love...is not jealous or conceited or proud (1 Corinthians 13:4 TEV). If you are angry, be sure that it is not a sinful anger. Never go to bed angry—don't give the devil that sort of foothold....Be kind to each other, be compassionate. Be as ready to forgive others as God for Christ's sake has forgiven you (Ephesians 4:26, 32 Phillips).

The Voice talks about—

Getting Ahead in Life

"One has to learn how to adapt. Right? This is the 20th century. One must be *realistic*!"

One Must Be *Realistic*

The Voice: We need to be
    in *the world*
    if we are ever
    going to
    change it
    Right?
    And I don't see
    how we can't help
    but become
    a significant part
    of *that world*
    if we are ever
    going to
    affect it
    Right?
    After all
    one has to learn
    how to adapt
    This is
    the 20th century!
    One must be
    realistic!

But *Another Voice* said:

What God the Father considers to be pure and genuine religion is this...to keep oneself from being corrupted by the world (James 1:27 TEV). Unfaithful people!
Don't you know that to be the world's friend means to be

God's enemy? Whoever wants to be the world's friend makes himself God's enemy (James 4:4 TEV). Do not love the world or anything that belongs to the world. If you love the world, you do not love the Father.... The world and everything in it that people desire is passing away; but he who does the will of God lives forever (1 John 2:15, 17 TEV).

Submission

The Voice: If there's one thing
that won't work
in our society
it's "submission"
to other people
That's especially true
in the business world
Otherwise
you'll never get ahead
It's certainly true
in marriage
For if you always yield
to the other person
you'll become
a milquetoast
with no integrity
or self-respect
Strive to win
and the other person
will grow along
with you
in the process

But *Another Voice* said:

Submit yourselves to one another because of your reverence for Christ (Ephesians 5:21 TEV). For the sake of the Lord submit yourselves to every human authority (1 Peter 2:13 TEV). Humble yourselves...under God's mighty hand, so that He will lift you up in His own good time (1 Peter 5:6 TEV).

On Wielding Power

The Voice: There's nothing wrong
with having power
and using it
in business
in administration
as a parent
Christ never condemned
rulers
or the rich
or soldiers
all of whom
wielded power
So if you
have a position
of authority
I say
God gave it
to you
Use it!
And enjoy
the feeling
of being
in control

But *Another Voice* said:

On a chosen day Herod put on his royal robes, sat on his throne, and made a speech to the people. "It isn't a man speaking, but a god!" they shouted. At once the angel of the Lord struck Herod down, because he did not give honor to God. He was eaten by worms and died (Acts 12:21-23 TEV). The Scripture says, "Whoever wants to boast must boast of what the Lord has done" (1 Corinthians 1:31 TEV). Do not cheat a poor and needy hired servant (Deuteronomy 24:14 TEV). Defend the rights of the poor and the orphans; be fair to the needy and the helpless (Psalm 82:3 TEV). Masters, give unto your servants that which is just and equal; knowing that ye also have a Master in heaven (Colossians 4:1 KJV).

(See Reflection 9)

Lifeless Garden Hoses?

The Voice: "You're going
          to make it
          on your own"
          So the song goes
          I believe
          that's true
          God helps those
          who help themselves
          He wants us
          to do our part
          He doesn't expect
          total dependency
          on Him
          where He just
          pumps His power

through us
like lifeless
garden hoses
So assert
your own ability
and integrity
and develop
the person
that is
you!

But *Another Voice* said:
     You do not belong to yourselves but to God; He
bought you for a price. So use your bodies for God's
glory (1 Corinthians 6:19-20 TEV). It is by God's grace
that you have been saved through faith. It is not the result
of your own efforts, but God's gift, so that no one can
boast about it (Ephesians 2:8-9 TEV). You can do nothing
without Me (John 15:5 TEV). It is no longer I who live, but
it is Christ who lives in me. This life that I live now, I live
by faith in the Son of God, who loved me and gave His
life for me (Galatians 2:20 TEV).

(See Reflection 10)

You Can Do It!

The Voice: I really like
          what many of those
          TV preachers say
          about becoming
          a better Christian
          "Believe in yourself

73

and you can do it"
"God will help you
get ahead"
"Think positively
and everything will
work out right
in your life"
I too believe
we should tap
the potential
God has placed
within us
That's Biblical
And that's practical!
A great team!
You and God!
Go to it!

But *Another Voice* said:

It is the Lord who gives wisdom; from Him come knowledge and understanding (Proverbs 2:6 TEV). Trust in the Lord with all your heart. Never rely on what you think you know. Remember the Lord in everything you do, and He will show you the right way (Proverbs 3:5-6 TEV). It is He that hath made us, and not we ourselves (Psalm 100:3 KJV). There is nothing in us that allows us to claim that we are capable of doing this work. The capacity we have comes from God (2 Corinthians 3:5 TEV).

Just a Job

The Voice: What drudgery
we all
have to
put up with
Ironing typing driving
Washing selling sewing
Digging fixing mixing
Working!
But it's all
necessary
to get those
good things
God wants us
to have
Right?

But *Another Voice* said:
It will be very hard for rich people to enter the kingdom of heaven. I repeat: it is much harder for a rich person to enter the kingdom of God than for a camel to go through the eye of a needle (Matthew 19:23-24 TEV). Whatever you do, whether you eat or drink, do it all for God's glory (1 Corinthians 10:31 TEV).

(See Reflection 11)

"Moving On Up!"

The Voice: Christ never did
put down rich people—
did He?

So I say
there's nothing wrong
in wanting that
bigger house
better car
higher-paying job
or more things
for the children
These are honest
human ambitions
God placed
within us
And He told us
to "work while it is day"
didn't He?
So strive to
improve your condition
Now
that's Biblical!

But *Another Voice* said:
    Be content with your pay (Luke 3:14 TEV). I have learned, in whatsoever state I am, therewith to be content (Philippians 4:11 KJV). Command those who are rich in the things of this life not to be proud, but to place their hope, not in such an uncertain thing as riches, but in God, who generously gives us everything for our enjoyment (1 Timothy 6:17 TEV). Store up riches for yourselves in heaven, where moths and rust cannot destroy, and robbers break in and steal. For your heart will always be where your riches are (Matthew 6:20-21 TEV).

(See Reflection 12)

The Voice talks about—

Doing All Right with God

"I think some people can make you *feel* bad when you really haven't done anything *that* bad at all. Shake off those negative feelings. Don't be so hard on yourself. Enjoy God's gift of a happy life for you."

Pray for the Poor

The Voice: It is very important
that you pray
for the souls
of poor people
Now of course
you should share with them
such things
as you can
But Christ said
"the poor you
shall always have with you"
And I think you see
the special kind
of grace and happiness
God gives them
to bear up
under trials and suffering
(Some even seem to be happier
than rich people!
Isn't that amazing!)
So I say
Help them
as you can
But care for your own family
(first to one's own
be true
as the Bible says)
And then
pray especially

for the spiritual condition
of the impoverished
and hope they will learn
the apostle Paul's prayer
that in whatsoever state
one is to be
content

But *Another Voice* said:

Suppose there are brothers or sisters who need clothes and don't have enough to eat. What good is there in your saying to them, "God bless you! Keep warm and eat well!"—if you don't give them the necessities of life? So it is with faith: if it is alone and includes no actions, then it is dead (James 2:15-17 TEV). If you refuse to listen to the cry of the poor, your own cry for help will not be heard (Proverbs 21:13 TEV). If a rich person sees his brother in need, yet closes his heart against his brother, how can he claim that he loves God? (1 John 3:17 TEV). Be not forgetful to entertain strangers: for thereby some have entertained angels unawares (Hebrews 13:2 KJV). When you give to the poor, it is like lending to the Lord, and the Lord will pay you back (Proverbs 19:17 TEV).

Doing OK with God

The Voice: Frankly I think
        things are going
        fairly well
        for you
        That's
        a pretty good sign
        that you are doing

OK with God
Right?
Otherwise He
in His ongoing love
would hold you back
a bit
Don't you think?
For He is always
watching over you
So if
life is going on
as usual
I think that's proof
that all is well
"God's in His heaven
All's right with the world"

But *Another Voice* said:

Be on watch, be alert, for you do not know when the time will come (Mark 13:33 TEV). Whoever thinks he is standing firm had better be careful that he does not fall (1 Corinthians 10:12 TEV).

(See Reflection 13)

Loosen Up!

The Voice: There's a big difference
between guilt
and a
"guilt complex"
I think some people
can make you

80

feel bad
when you really
haven't done anything
that bad at all
(We all make mistakes)
So don't let that
badgering conscience
or nagging "friend"
or overbearing preacher
get you down
You are a free person
living in God's grace
Loosen up
Shake off those
negative feelings
Don't be
so hard on yourself
Enjoy God's gift
of a happy life
for you

But *Another Voice* said:
    I know that good does not live in me—that is, in my human nature. For even though the desire to do good is in me, I am not able to do it (Romans 7:18 TEV). All of us have been sinful; even our best actions are filthy through and through (Isaiah 64:6 TEV). I have sinned against You—only against You—and done what You consider evil. So You are right in judging me; You are justified in condemning me (Psalm 51:4 TEV).

(See Reflection 14)

81

Congratulations!

The Voice: So some prosperity
has finally come
your way
You deserve it!
And you've earned it
It's good to see
you are finally
secure
Now you are better known
have more acquaintances
and feel more important
I think
that's great
Congratulations!

But *Another Voice* said:

Rich people always think they are wise, but a poor person who has insight into character knows better (Proverbs 28:11 TEV). Never boast about tomorrow. You don't know what will happen between now and then (Proverbs 27:1 TEV). Be awake and sober (1 Thessalonians 5:6 TEV).

(See Reflection 15)

They Blew It

The Voice: I've always
been impressed
by the many people
in the Bible who

really blew it
Adam and Eve—disobedience
The children of Israel—idolatry, etc.
David—adultery
Solomon—apostasy
Jonah—dereliction of duty
Peter—betrayal
Martha—inverted priorities
et cetera
But God
forgave all of them
What a patient
loving
bighearted
God we have!
Now I'm not
saying He's
"in the business"
of forgiveness
But it's comforting
to know
he'll always
take us back

But *Another Voice* said:

Keep your faith and a clear conscience. Some men have not listened to their conscience and have made a ruin of their faith (1 Timothy 1:19 TEV). My fellow believers, be careful that no one among you has a heart so evil and unbelieving that he will turn away from the living God. Instead, in order that none of you be deceived by sin and become stubborn, you must help one another every day.... For we are all partners with Christ if we hold firmly to the end the confidence we had at the beginning (Hebrews 3:12-14 TEV). Be on your guard...so that you will not be led away by the errors of lawless people and fall from your safe position (2 Peter 3:17 TEV). If we confess our sins to God, He will keep His promise and do what is right; He will forgive us our sins and purify us from all our wrongdoing (1 John 1:9 TEV).

The Voice talks about—

Those Overcommitted Christians

"Some Christians may have it easy with their little faith formulas. But life is tough. Hang in there. You've got *my* sympathy."

Busyness, Bazaars, and Building Programs

The Voice: *Of course a person*
should go to church
But don't become
one of those
"overcommitted Christians"
who turn other people off
who might otherwise
join the church
Take a calm look
at what's really
going on
in that parish
Do you want to
get involved in
busyness? bazaars?
building programs?
paying off debts?
listening to lectures?
just
maintaining an institution?
Think twice
You can be
a Christian on your own
Oh don't cut yourself
completely off
But keep cool
Learn Bible study
on your own

And maybe you
can help others
do the same thing
too

But *Another Voice* said:
Whenever you possibly can, do good to those who need it (Proverbs 3:27 TEV). Help carry one another's burdens, and in this way you will obey the law of Christ (Galatians 6:2 TEV). Let us not give up the habit of meeting together, as some are doing. Instead, let us encourage one another all the more, since you see that the Day of the Lord is coming nearer (Hebrews 10:25 TEV).

Share More of Yourself

The Voice: People never grow
            if all they get
            is praise
            I think that's true
            in the church also
            Those hymn-singers
            will never mature
            if they never receive
            helpful loving criticism
            How many a congregation
            has been improved
            by the infusion of
            fresh blood
            new life
            different insights

You can make
your contribution also
Don't be a follower
Be a leader
God has given you
the ability
God bless
your efforts

But *Another Voice* said:

Never let yourself think you are wiser than you are (Proverbs 3:7 TEV). The most stupid fool is better off than someone who thinks he is wise when he is not (Proverbs 26:12 TEV). Arrogance will bring your downfall, but if you are humble, you will be respected (Proverbs 29:23 TEV). Have the same concern for everyone. Do not think of yourselves as wise (Romans 12:16 TEV).

GOD IS LOVE!

The Voice: Did you ever notice
how much a congregation
secretly enjoys it
when a pastor
"comes down hard" on them
in a sermon?
(Actually they wish
the Johnsons
had been in church
They needed it!)
That's rather sad though

God is not
a God of wrath
and judgment
That's an
outmoded
misconception
of our heavenly Father
GOD IS LOVE
Now
that's
Biblical!

But *Another Voice* said:
The wrath of God is revealed from heaven against all ungodliness and wickedness of men who by their wickedness suppress the truth (Romans 1:18 RSV). Do not let anyone deceive you with foolish words; it is because of these very things that God's anger will come upon those who do not obey Him (Ephesians 5:6 TEV). Do not deceive yourselves; no one makes a fool of God (Galatians 6:7 TEV).

You Are Not Albert Schweitzer

The Voice: God doesn't expect you
to be some kind of
super-Christian
like
Albert Schweitzer or
Mother Teresa
or to take a chance
with your life

in a jungle
or a slum
We are given
different gifts
You can pray
for the underprivileged
and the oppressed
give generously
to your church
or community organizations
pray and help to alleviate
world hunger
with a generous check
But you need not
become one of those
(really self-serving)
"Christian" activists
living in a depressed area
to prove they are
"real Christians"
To really *be one*
Christ calls you
to serve
where you are at
So don't let
those "self-sacrificing types"
get you down
They have their reward
Publicity!
Just what they want
You have yours
A quiet
dignified witness
in your own
community

But *Another Voice* said:
Our love should not be just words and talk; it must
be true love, which shows itself in action (1 John 3:18
TEV). Never tell your neighbor to wait until tomorrow if
you can help him now (Proverbs 3:28 TEV). If you want
to be happy, be kind to the poor; it is a sin to despise
anyone (Proverbs 14:21 TEV).

Faith Formulas

The Voice: I see other people
are trying to push
their ideas on you
(especially religious)
They say
"Have faith"
"Everything will
be all right"
"God cares for you"
(Of course He does)
But what works out
for them in life
may not work out
for you
They don't have to live
your *life!*
Each one of us
is different
Unique!
Some Christians
may have it easy
with their little
faith formulas

But
life is tough
Hang in there
You've got
my *sympathy*

But *Another Voice* said:
   Your Father in heaven...makes His sun to shine on bad and good people alike, and gives rain to those who do good and to those who do evil (Matthew 5:45 TEV). I alone know the plans I have for you, plans to bring you prosperity and not disaster, plans to bring about the future you hope for. Then you will call to Me. You will come and pray to Me, and I will answer you. You will seek Me, and you will find Me because you will seek Me with all your heart (Jeremiah 29:11-13 TEV).

The Voice talks about—

Considering Divorce

"Why not admit you can never be what the other person wants you to be? Why feel you can never be any good with anyone else if you couldn't make it with your partner?"

I Don't Need Counseling

The Voice: "Getting counseling
is the beginning
of the divorce"
is what he said
"We can—
with God's help—
work this out
on our own"
Don't you agree?
How meddlesome
and cool
and smug
and arrogant
those advice-givers
can become!
Don't you agree?
I say
talk it over
keep trying
to work it out
together
You can do it
on your own

But *Another Voice* said:
Pride leads to destruction, and arrogance to downfall (Proverbs 16:18 TEV). You may think everything you do is right, but the Lord judges your motives (Proverbs 16:2 TEV).

(See Reflection 16)

1 + 1 = 1?

The Voice: They say
in marriage
one plus one
equals one
But I would
resist that
cute equation
Do you want
to become
a mere shadow
of your partner?
Instead express
your individuality
Resist conformity
And as you assert your
unique identity
a truly exciting
interplay
of two quite different
personalities
can be enjoyed

But *Another Voice* said:

Live in harmony with one another; do not be haughty . . . never be conceited (Romans 12:16 RSV). Be completely united, with only one thought and one purpose (1 Corinthians 1:10 TEV). The God of love and peace will be with you (2 Corinthians 13:11 TEV). I urge you...[share] the same love, and [be] one in soul and mind (Philippians 2:2 TEV). You must all have the same attitude and the same feelings; love one another...and be kind and humble with one another (1 Peter 3:8 TEV). Submit yourselves to one another because of your reverence for Christ (Ephesians 5:21 TEV).

The Fire in the Bedroom

The Voice: A woman
down there
(high-spirited
to be sure)
said she always
loved to win
in a discussion
with her husband
And although he
would finally
give in to her
she always
made it up to him
in bed
It worked!
Try it sometime
It can work
for you too
and keep the

fire going in
the bedroom
and the spice alive
in your
relationship

But *Another Voice* said:
Do not use harmful words, but only helpful words, the kind that build up and provide what is needed, so that what you say will do good to those who hear you (Ephesians 4:29 TEV). Love must be completely sincere. Hate what is evil, hold on to what is good. Love one another warmly...and be eager to show respect for one another (Romans 12:9-10 TEV). In all things you yourself must be an example....Be sincere and serious (Titus 2:7 TEV). Our love should not be just words and talk; it must be true love, which shows itself in action (1 John 3:18 TEV).

Fulfillment Outside Your Marriage

The Voice: When hopes and dreams
diminish
(especially in middle age)
and the closeness
you once had
with your partner
has faded away
it's too late
to think divorce
Rather
reach out
make new friends

let the
undiscovered "you"
blossom out
in new relationships
and new challenges
Find excitement
in different work
a new hobby
Tap the unused talents
deep within you
Be yourself
in what can be
a whole new world
of adventure
for you!
Go to it!

But *Another Voice* said:

A man away from home is like a bird away from its nest (Proverbs 27:8 TEV). Do not deny yourselves to each other, unless you first agree to do so for a while in order to spend your time in prayer; but then resume normal marital relations. In this way you will be kept from giving in to Satan's temptation because of your lack of self-control (1 Corinthians 7:5 TEV). If you do not forgive others, your Father in heaven will not forgive the wrongs you have done (Mark 11:26 TEV).

(See Reflection 17)

Time for Divorce?

The Voice: Do you know
what it is like
to live with
the perfect partner?
I think
there are times
when the loss
of self-respect
and identity
and constant sense
of failure
are worse
than divorce
Why live
in constant guilt?
Why not admit
you can never be
what the other wants
you to be?
Why feel
you can never be
any good
with anyone else
if you couldn't make it
with your partner?
Sometimes
one must choose
the lesser
of two evils
and discover
the freedom
of finally being
yourself

But *Another Voice* said:

The steadfast love of the Lord never ceases, His mercies never come to an end; they are new every morning (Lamentations 3:22-23 RSV). Love is patient and kind; it is not jealous or conceited or proud; love is not ill-mannered or selfish or irritable; love does not keep a record of wrongs.... Love never gives up; and its faith, hope, and patience never fail (1 Corinthians 13:4,7 TEV). God, be merciful to me a sinner! (Luke 18:13 RSV)

The Voice talks about—

The Past, Present, and Future

"The debris of the past in the river of your life is not necessarily of your own making. So live with yourself as you are. Don't try to be something you are not. *Be you!*"

Happiness Is Coming Your Way!

The Voice: Your life has been
> *very interesting but it*
> *is only the beginning*
> *of what*
> *is going to happen*
> *to you!*
> *I see great*
> *untapped possibilities*
> *ahead of you*
> *dreams fulfilled*
> *beyond your wildest*
> *imagination!*
> *God will*
> *come through*
> *for you*
> *He never*
> *lets*
> *us*
> *down*

But *Another Voice* said:

Never boast about tomorrow. You don't know what will happen between now and then (Proverbs 27:1 TEV). Be alert, be on watch! Your enemy, the devil, roams around like a roaring lion, looking for someone to devour (1 Peter 5:8 TEV).

Quiet Dignified Resignation

The Voice: Life is rough
(as a Christian
you must admit that)
World conflicts and disasters
Oppression and injustice
Your loss
of security
Illness
Accidents
The onset of age
Alienation from others
The earlier dreams
of love and hope and success
not fulfilled
What to do
in the face
of all this?
Well the Scripture says
and I believe
we need to learn
a kind of
quiet dignified resignation
as the early Christians did
Their example and integrity
are to be
emulated
Learn from them
God gives
the grace

But *Another Voice* said:..

Being cheerful keeps you healthy. It is slow death to be gloomy all the time (Proverbs 17:22 TEV). Tears may flow in the night, but joy comes in the morning (Psalm 30:5 TEV). Until now you have not asked for anything in My name; ask and you will receive, so that your happiness may be complete (John 16:24 TEV). For God's kingdom is not a matter of eating and drinking, but of the righteousness, peace, and joy which the Holy Spirit gives (Romans 14:17 TEV).

Facing Death?

The Voice: So your friend
is facing death
How sad!
But how involved
and complicated
death is
I suggest
just turning it all
over to God
and let Him
handle it
He's a big God
Don't ask
so many questions
Your friend
is a good person
God is
in control
So
don't worry

But *Another Voice* said:

How happy are those servants whose master finds them awake and ready when he returns! (Luke 12:37 TEV). Be alert, stand firm in the faith, be brave, be strong (1 Corinthians 16:13 TEV). Be persistent in prayer, and keep alert as you pray, giving thanks to God (Colossians 4:2 TEV). It is by God's grace that you have been saved through faith. It is not the result of your own efforts, but God's gift, so that no one can boast about it (Ephesians 2:8-9 TEV).

Change for the Sake of Change?

The Voice: I say
> *(don't you?)*
> *that we should*
> *hang on to*
> *the old values*
> *and resist the pressures*
> *of so-called*
> *"social progress"*
> *much of which*
> *is a thinly disguised*
> *attempt to promote*
> *a relativistic morality*
> *social unrest*
> *and it leads to*
> *the loss of*
> *the truths*
> *we've always*
> *believed in*

Change
for change's sake
is unwise
The past
must never be
dishonored

But *Another Voice* said:

Anyone who starts to plow and then keeps looking back is of no use for the kingdom of God (Luke 9:62 TEV). All I can say is this: forgetting what is behind me, and reaching out for what lies ahead, I press towards the goal to win the prize which is God's call to the life above, in Christ Jesus (Philippians 3:13-14 NEB). Behold, I make all things new (Revelation 21:5 RSV).

Think on Things Eternal

The Voice: Are you tired?
     weary?
     depressed?
     Then concentrate only
     on the joys
     of eternal rest
     Bliss supernal
     in the presence
     of God
     What joy!
     I say
     strive daily
     to focus your mind

solely
on heaven
Withdraw yourself
from the world
and you can
rise above
the pain
the agony
the suffering that
this present life
brings
Think about
things eternal
all the time
God will bless you
for that

But *Another Voice* said:

Remember your Creator while you are still young, before those dismal days and years come when you will say, "I don't enjoy life" (Ecclesiastes 12:1 TEV). Work hard at whatever you do, because there will be no action, no thought, no knowledge, no wisdom in the world of the dead—and that is where you are going (Ecclesiastes 9:10 TEV). This is the day which the Lord has made; let us rejoice and be glad in it (Psalm 118:24 RSV).

(See Reflection 18)

The Voice talks about—

Coping with the Daily Drag

"How you tire of everyone around you who wants to use you for selfish purposes and designs! What new opportunity beckons you? Where is the fresh start you so richly deserve?"

Waiting for Help

The Voice: Do you get discouraged
    like I do
    when you finally try
    to read the Bible
    on your own?
    How often one
    gets confused
    and it's so hard
    to understand
    I suggest prayer instead
    or reading good
    Christian novels
    When they finally
    devise an easy way
    to interpret
    the Bible
    I'll be ready

But *Another Voice* said:

Foolish people! How long do you want to be foolish? How long will you enjoy making fun of knowledge? Will you never learn? Listen when I reprimand you; I will give you good advice and share my knowledge with you (Proverbs 1:22-23 TEV). Learn what I teach you and never forget what I tell you to do.... If you do, you will know what it means to fear the Lord and you will succeed in learning about God (Proverbs 2:1, 5 TEV). If you refuse good advice, you are asking for trouble; follow it and you are safe (Proverbs 13:13 TEV). Pay attention to what you are taught, and you will be successful; trust in the Lord and you will be happy (Proverbs 16:20 TEV). Study the Scriptures (John 5:39 TEV).

(See Reflection 19)

Family Devotions

The Voice: Do you honestly know
of one family
in your acquaintance
that has a
consistent time
for family devotions
and sticks to it?
Not to feel guilty!
Now I say
it's just impossible
in our *culture*
and with the
pressures
schedules
commuting
demands on us
of all kinds
to make it happen
At least we can
pray together
at meal time
if we're
all there!

But *Another Voice* said:
Do all this in prayer, asking for God's help. Pray on every occasion, as the Spirit leads. For this reason keep alert and never give up; pray always for all God's people (Ephesians 6:18 TEV). Pray at all times (1 Thessalonians 5:17 TEV). Confess your sins to one another and pray for one another, so that you will be healed (James 5:16 TEV).

They Just Don't Understand

The Voice: "I know just
how you feel"
What insipid nonsense
from "well-meaning
Christian friends"
No one can ever
fully know
the pain and hurt
to yourself
I say
Keep grief
burdens doubts
inside you
No one else
can ever really understand
I say
just
"take it to
the Lord
in prayer"

But *Another Voice* said:

Help carry one another's burdens, and in this way you will obey the law of Christ (Galatians 6:2 TEV). We who are strong in the faith ought to help the weak to carry their burdens. We should not please ourselves. Instead, we should all please our brothers for their own good, in order to build them up in the faith (Romans 15:1-2 TEV). Is there anyone who is sick? He should send for the church elders, who will pray for him and rub olive oil on him in the name of the Lord. . . . Confess your sins to one another and pray for one another, so that you will be healed. The prayer of a good person has a powerful effect (James 5:14, 16 TEV).

Tired? Move Out!

The Voice: Ah
    how hard it is
    to live with others.
    who always want
    to control *you*
    How you tire
    of every person
    around you
    who wants
    to use you
    for their own
    purposes and designs!
    Now!—
    What new tack
    can you take
    in your life?

What new opportunity
beckons you?
Where is the
fresh start
you so richly
deserve?
What exciting adventure
could now be yours
if you only
dared
in faith
to "move out"
and enjoy
the long-delayed freedom
Christ wants you
to have?

But *Another Voice* said:

But you, my friends, already know this. Be on your guard, then, so that you will not be led away by the errors of lawless people and fall from your safe position. But continue to grow in the grace and knowledge of our Lord and Savior Jesus Christ. To Him be the glory, now and forever! Amen (2 Peter 3:17-18 TEV).

Most Sincerely Yours—*The Voice*

The Voice: You have heard
my voice now
many times
I am your friend

113

I have tried
to help you
Trust me
Believe in me
For I come
from your *world*
your *friends*
and your *inner soul*
I am only suggesting
what is best for you
So listen once more
God made you
Be yourself
Stop letting others
around you
squeeze you
into their own mold
The Bible says
you are free in Christ
Be *free then*
Exercise your individuality
And enjoy your freedom
You'll hear from me
again soon
Most *sincerely yours*
The Voice*

*From *I Hear Two Voices* (Concordia, 1983), p.99.

Epilog: The Christian Responds

But as *The Voice* stopped speaking (only for a moment, of course) *The Christian* suddenly said:

"So it was really you, Satan, all the time! *You*, with your pack of lies! I recognize you now, Prince of Hell, for the Deceiver you really are! Everything you have said has only been your ghastly design for my demise and downfall.

"Not that I can say 'The devil made me do it!' and blame you for the evil you have so often conned me into doing, but I now see your cunning rationalizations exposed. Get going now, Satan! In the name of Jesus Christ, leave me! Get out with your pack of lies and leave me alone with my true Master, my Savior, Jesus Christ. In His name, I command you, get behind me!

"I've had enough of your tricks and deceits.

"And now, by the power of the Holy Spirit, I turn to You, Lord! "It's really been *You*, all the time. I've doubted You. I've failed You. I've grieved You. Your Son, Jesus Christ, died on the cross for my sins—my sins of self-seeking, of hurting others, of ignoring Your call to service and sacrifice.

"But I love You, Lord. Forgive me, Lord. Now let me hear Your Voice again, Lord!

"It's really been *You*, all the time!

"Jesus, Master, have mercy upon me.

"I am home again.

"Home again to stay."

And *God* replied:

"And it was you also, *you*, My beloved child, all the time! I, your Father—who woos you, is grieved by you, who chases you, forgives you, is again disappointed in you, but still wants you to remain My child.

"In spite of all your prodigal wandering in the barnyard of life, now I want you at My side, at My right hand, in the place of honor at My festal table!

"Come! Take My hand!

"Let's go in together."

And as *The Christian* and God walked together, God said:

"He's always there
to tempt you
in a million different ways
even when you sleep
in the fantasy world
of your subconscious
But I overcame him
for you
I met his tests
three times
in the person of
My Son
I promise you
the same victory is yours
through faith in Him
So remember that although
Satan never sleeps
I don't
either!"*

*Matthew 4:1-11   1 John 5:4   Psalm 121:4

*From "Satan Never Sleeps" in *You Promised Me, God!* (Concordia, 1980), p. 38, by the author—a book that is in the opposite vein of *Voices and Choices*. There the *Voice* is that of God Himself sharing some of His thousands of promises to the Christian.

Author's Postscript to the Reader

When you heard *The Voice* talking at times, you may have thought in response: "Well, what's wrong with that? That's the way I've been thinking for some time. In fact, that's what most of my friends say—and they are Christians, too!"

Or you may have mused: "Well, frankly, that's about the only way you can get along in the world today—at least in the dog-eat-dog world *I* live in!"

And so you have disagreed with my intimation that the statement of *The Voice* was intrinsically demonic. Good! In this disagreement between what I have written and your point of view—that of a reader—there can be creative growth as we together search the Scriptures to see if these things are really so (see Acts 17:11).

What I have tried to do is show the subtle way in which Satan, the world around us, and most of all, our own sinful self woo us into rationalizing our thoughts and deeds. It is this sinful self with which we need to cope—and to recognize the many ways in which Satan tries to work through it to defeat us. For *The Voice* wants us to follow our old nature. Whereas *Another Voice* calls us to be a "new creation"—a "little Christ" (See 2 Corinthians 5:17).

At this point the Christian needs to concentrate on the *power* supply, the *Source*. "Christ is in you" (Colossians 1:27 TEV; see also 1 John 4:17 Phillips). In the means of grace God gives us the power to overcome Satan and his hosts of evil angels who confront us. (God is not Satan's counterpart. The archangel Michael is. And he has hosts of angels on his side, too. *Your* side. God is still in control.)

The means of grace are the Word of God and the Sacraments. Search the Scriptures daily—with an open mind and a penitent heart; by the power of the Holy Spirit relive your baptism every day (see Romans 6:3-4); go to the Lord's Table frequently and joyfully, there to receive the body and blood of Christ—the Christ *for* us, who is now the Christ *in* us—forgiving our sins.

"Resist the devil and he will flee from you," says the Scripture (James 4:7 RSV). And here most of all we need to study our Lord's own response to the devil's temptations in the wilderness.

Note how Jesus cut Satan down three times with the sword of the Spirit—the Holy Scriptures. Satan misquoted Scripture to Him (as *The Voice* does a number of times in the vignettes). But Christ said *rather* "It is written!"—and with the power of God's true Word sent the devil away.

That must be our ultimate weapon against Satan. *"It is written!"* There is *power* in the *written* Word of Scripture as it is "cried out" (Luther)—and that is why Christ did so repeatedly. It is the power of God unto salvation for all who believe (Romans 1:16). With it on our lips we can say: *"Go away, Satan!"*

To say that, we must know the Scriptures. Satan will leave us for a while, but he will return again—in a different guise—and we must be ready for him.

It is my prayer that you will meditate again and again on what *Another Voice* says in these vignettes, for they are the inspired words of God Himself in the Holy Scriptures. With me, "examine yourself," as you search out what the will of the Lord is for your life. And may the Holy Spirit guide you in your actions, as you "choose this day whom you will serve" (Joshua 24:15 RSV).

Further Uses for This Book

Beyond use for personal meditation, this volume is adaptable as a "chancel drama" or for presentation to smaller groups—youth gatherings, men's and women's meetings—choosing the number of vignettes for length as desired.

For larger groups, a *Prompter* (stage center rear) could read the *Introduction*. Then the *Prompter* would announce the title of each piece, and say: "*The Voice.*" *The Voice* (stage right front) reads the vignette (not too rapidly), after which the *Prompter* says: "But *Another Voice* said—" *Another Voice* (stage left front) reads the response—again, slowly. A very brief pause may be helpful after each *individual* Scripture passage—although a rationale of progression has been attempted in the sequence of the passages. To retain the "flow" of the passages, the Scripture references (e.g., "John 3:16 TEV") might well be omitted.

After *Another Voice* concludes each time, there might be a *brief* moment of silence for the group's reflection. Then the *Prompter* announces the next piece.

The *Epilog* may be read by the *Prompter*. Or, someone playing the part of *The Christian* (who could have been standing stage center front all the time) could read the responses in the *Epilog* to both *Satan* and *God*. Then the *Prompter* could respond with the final portion ("Satan Never Sleeps") as the two walk together stage center back—towards the altar.

After the drama, as time permits, the following questions could be offered for group discussion. For this dialog, the "cast" might well be primed on the content of the "Author's Postscript to the Reader" and the "Reflections" sections to give added insights both on where there is disagreement regarding the intimated evil in what *The Voice* is always saying and on how the Christian copes with *The Voice* in his or her daily life.

In smaller groups, if the vignettes are discussed individually, it might be helpful for *The Voice* to repeat its original challenge, after the Scripture verses have been read, to reintensify the theme as it is then thrown open for group discussion.

Dialog Follow-up Questions

1. What do you see as the essential attitude / approach of *The Voice?*
2. Where, especially for you, does *The Voice* come from—from within yourself, from your friends, what you see, read, or where?
3. What do you see as the essential nature of *Another Voice?*
4. Where do you feel the Christian's greatest vulnerabilities lie?
5. What are the Christian's greatest resources in coping with *The Voice?*
6. When did you feel that what *The Voice* was saying "wasn't all that bad"?
7. How does a Christian *decide* which *Voice* to listen to—and follow? And in what ways can the Christian better listen to *Another Voice?*

Reflections

1. *How Modest!* "If you think you are not conceited, it means you are very conceited" (C.S. Lewis).

2. *The Balancing Act.* Maybe you are balanced. Good. But it's a daily test to remain "unspotted from the world" (see James 1:27 KJV). Are you really ready for the next disguise *The Voice* will use when it tries to deceive you where you work?

3. *How Can I Pray?* If you are searching the Bible daily— especially the Psalms—you can learn to pray by asking, "Lord, please move me to *respond* to Your Word." Then meditate again on what He has just said to you in Scripture. There *are* Christians who are glad to help improve your prayer life, too. And if you ever fall asleep while you pray, well, my grandma always used to say: "Don't worry. The Holy Spirit will finish your prayers for you!"

4. *It's Not Your Fault.* It may well be that you have a faith problem and not a physical one. But you are not alone. The Great Physician is ready to heal you and lift you up with the balm of his healing love and care.

5. *Me Feel Happy? Ha!* Satan just can't stand honest Christian joy, especially the happy singing of praises to God. (Peter even sang in prison; Acts 16:25) Next time you are depressed, sing—and just see what happens!

6. *Your Hidden Talents.* The source of whatever good we do is God, not ourselves. What is the *very first* thought you had this morning? Did you think of yourself and *your* plans for the day, or *God's mercies*? (See Lamentations 3:23) What a gracious, benevolent, and self-giving God we have!

7. *How Rude!* So people do interrupt you. So styles of conversation are different than yours. But do you "talk in paragraphs" (as I often do!)? "There is only one way the Christian can come into the presence of other people. He/she will learn how to listen and listen completely" (Harry A. DeWire, as quoted in the author's *Bound to Be Free: The Quest for Inner Freedom* (Seattle: Morse Press, 1981), p.93.

8. *A Fine Command of Language.* Yes and no. We certainly need to develop the skill of "active listening." But ultimately we are compelled by the love of Christ in us to *articulate* the Good News of the Gospel: "In Christ God was reconciling the world to himself, not counting their trespasses against them, and entrusting to us the message of reconciliation" (2 Corinthians 5:19 RSV).

9. *On Wielding Power.* The feeling of power may lead to the misuse of power. Has power *ever* corrupted you?

10. *Lifeless Garden Hoses?* Christ calls us to *respond* to the Gospel and to live a life of good works—*but* that others may see this to glorify *God.* The fruit of the Spirit in our lives is sown by *Him*—not by us (see Galatians 5—6).

11. *Just a Job.* "Occupation" is the job you have. But "vocation" is work—*whatever it is*—done to the glory of God. As Donald R. Heiges says in *The Christian's Calling* (Philadelphia: Muhlenberg Press, 1958), p. 19: "Only when [people] believe in God can they perceive substantial meaning in existence; only when [people] can perceive meaning can they be captivated by vocation; and when [people] are captivated by vocation, they can live above despair to the glory of God."

12. *"Moving On Up!"* Of course being rich is not wrong. When the Lord blesses you with riches, more is required of you in giving. The question is: what are you really living—and dying—for—right now? What *new* and

different snares may *The Voice* be using to catch you today? Christ will give you the vision to recognize them.

13. *Doing OK with God.* "[For God] to watch a [person] doing something is not to make [the person] do it" (C. S. Lewis, *The Screwtape Letters* [Fleming H. Revell Co., 1976], p. 170).

14. *Loosen Up!* There *is* a difference between guilt and a "guilt complex." But for the person who feels no guilt or *daily need* for repentance at all, Martin Luther's words aptly apply: (1) First, put your hand in your bosom, and see if you are still warm. (2) Look around and see if you are still in the world, and remember that there is no end of sin and trouble. (3) Third (that being the case) remember that you will certainly have the devil near you, who with his lying and murdering, day and night, will let you have no peace at all. ("Christian Questions with Their Answers," paraphrased, *The Small Catechism*).

15. *Congratulations!* If "prosperity" has come your way, have you "found your place in the world" or has the "world found its place in you"? (C. S. Lewis, *The Screwtape Letters* [Fleming H. Revell Co., 1976], p. 130).

16. *I Don't Need Counseling.* There are times when we must swallow our pride, admit our own weaknesses, and get the help of others who have an objectivity that we have lost. They may also have an insight into Scripture and the guidance of the Holy Spirit that we sorely need. Continuing to just muddle along on your own with the same failure to communicate *can* lead to even more alienation. There are Christians—and counselors—who do want to help you—and who can.

17. *Fulfillment Outside Your Marriage.* Never "give up" on your spouse. God never gives up on you.

18. *Think on Things Eternal.* Of course. But note Paul's balance—and where he ends up in Philippians 1:23-26. He decided that it was more important to stay

alive and serve his flock. Besides the comfort of eternal rest there is also Christ's call to the adventure of dynamic and creative living.

19. *Waiting for Help.* There *are* groups and individual Christians ready to help you in meaningful Bible study. And the Bible study aids available today are countless. Just visit a Christian book store.

Special thanks to Paul E. Johnson for several insights from his helpful book *The Middle Years* (Philadelphia: Fortress Press, 1971).

BE ALERT,
> BE ON WATCH!
YOUR ENEMY, THE DEVIL,
> ROAMS AROUND LIKE A ROARING LION,
LOOKING FOR SOMEONE TO DEVOUR.
> BE FIRM IN YOUR FAITH AND RESIST
> HIM,
BECAUSE YOU KNOW THAT YOUR FELLOW
BELIEVERS
> IN ALL THE WORLD ARE GOING
> THROUGH
THE SAME KIND OF SUFFERINGS.

BUT AFTER YOU HAVE SUFFERED
FOR A LITTLE WHILE,
THE GOD OF GRACE, WHO CALLS YOU
TO SHARE HIS ETERNAL GLORY IN UNION
WITH CHRIST,
WILL HIMSELF PERFECT YOU,
AND GIVE YOU
FIRMNESS,
STRENGTH, AND
A SURE FOUNDATION.
TO HIM BE THE POWER FOREVER!
AMEN.

1 Peter 5:8-11 TEV

IT IS NOT
SINGLE VICTORIES
BUT PERSEVERANCE
THAT COUNTS

—Basilea Schlink: